Scot land the best

PETER IRVINE

exclusive edition for

THE SCOTSMAN

Author and journalist Pete Irvine is also Scotland's leading-edge event organizer. His company, Unique Events, created Edinburgh's annual Hogmanay Programme in 1993 (the year that he started this book); it has become the world's biggest New Year's celebration. He's also the artistic director of many of Scotland's major public events.

He received the Silver Thistle Award for his 'outstanding contribution to tourism in Scotland' and the MBE for services to Edinburgh. In 2008 he received an honorary doctorate from the Open University.

This edition has been produced exclusively for *The Scotsman* by Collins, an imprint of
HarperCollinsPublishers
77-85 Fulham Palace Road
London W6 8JB

www.collins.co.uk

This edition published in 2010
Text © Peter Irvine 2009

The author asserts the moral right to be identified as the author of this work

ISBN 978-0-00-786323-5

Material extracted from *Scotland the Best* published by Collins in 2009
ISBN 978-0-00-731965-7
Text © Peter Irvine 2009

Produced by The Printer's Devil, Glasgow

Printed and bound in Great Britain by
Clays, St Ives plc

Contents

I can't believe I've finished it again, never mind that we've reached the 10th edition of *Scotland the Best*. It's published every two years (though it was consecutive in the first three) so the 10th edition happily falls in 2010. To mark the event, there's a new section, 'My Top 10 for 2010', and a new email address so you can contact me directly (see below).

Ten editions is a fair length of time to observe and record both the changes in the Scotland that we live in and the experience we offer visitors. Most things have improved immeasurably (although we won't talk about the traffic). Where once good food was a rarity outside the city, there has been a marked proliferation in restaurants and hotels that are worth recommending at all levels. Once again, I like to think I've found them all. Everything from fish and chips to twee tearooms have come a long way from the days of lard and boiled-ham sandwiches. And though in Scotland we debate this endlessly, we have moved on from the less-than-welcoming, 'you'll have had your tea' attitude that once prevailed. Having covered the country from the far north beaches to the Solway coast, I honestly believe that Scotland, as in so many things, punches well above its weight. When it comes to accessible opening hours, local sourcing of ingredients and creative home cookery, we do excel.

Since the first edition I've tried to convey the many ways of appreciating a landscape: looking at it, driving through it, walking, swimming outdoors, watching birds, wild camping. In many ways, Scotland has led the way in the development of eco-tourism from those very first days when ospreys appeared at Loch Garten in 1954. Now there are more ways than ever of enjoying the outdoors. These categories, like all the others, have been updated for this new edition.

New readers should know that this is not a book about all the options – it only registers and commends the best of what there is. We don't venture into the mediocre even if that's all there is. Yet no matter how I strive to raise the bar in each edition, there is more rather than less that demands to be included. I try to be completely compre-hensive and embrace and include anywhere that deserves recognition. But the book is big enough already and it's supposed to be something that you can carry easily with you in your car or in your backpack so in this edition I've removed a couple of categories that I think people don't use as much.

Space – or the lack of it – dictates that while this little edition gives a flavour of *Scotland the Best*, much has to be omitted. This doesn't just mean entries themselves: ways of navigating the pages as you travel the country – notably by maps and by cross-references, which can tell you, for example, about a good pub in the area while you're out on your walk – haven't crossed over from the main book.

Clearly more and more people get the information they need from the internet and their mobile phone. I don't think (and I hope I'm right) that this makes a guidebook like this redundant. Indeed, it complements all the other forms of instant information; it is a complete and personal guide. However, it is time to allow a more direct commu-nication with readers who want to offer feedback so there's now an email address to write to and I hope you'll use it. From the volume of old-fashioned letters that I cur-rently get, I know this will unleash a deluge of responses from people who like a particular place and think I should know about it or have had a rubbish dinner at somewhere I've recommended and want to complain. That will be great but please don't expect me to reply to all. Everything will be logged and checked and in two year's time I will be going everywhere in Scotland again armed with all your information.

In the meantime, enjoy this Scotland in a new decade.

Pete Irvine
Edinburgh
December 2009
stb@lumison.co.uk

The Ticks

All places listed here are notable in some way; those which are outstanding have been 'awarded' a tick.

✓ Amongst the very best in Scotland

✓✓ Amongst the best (of its type) in the UK

✓✓✓ Amongst the best (of its type) in the world, or simply unique

Listings generally are not in an order of merit although if there is one outstanding item it will always be at the top of the page and this obviously includes anything which has been given a tick.

The Codes

These are the codes you will find listed beside many of the entries in this little book.

ATMOS indicates a place whose special atmosphere is an attraction in itself.

☕ signifies a notable café.

ECO denotes a place with an active 'green' agenda (eg, energy-saving policies, organic food).

HS Under the care of Historic Scotland.
Standard hours are: Apr-end Sep 7 days 9.30am-5.30pm. Oct-Mar Mon-Sat 9.30am-4.30pm. Some variations with individual properties; call 0131 668 8831 to check. All HS properties carry admission. www.historic-scotland.gov.uk

NTS Under the care of the National Trust for Scotland. Hours vary. Admission. www.nts.org.uk

RSPB Under the care of the Royal Society for the Protection of Birds.

Walk & Cycling Codes

Walks in this book have a series of codes; for example:

> *3-10KM   BIKES/ XBIKES/ MTBIKES*
> *CIRC/ XCIRC   1-A-1*

3-10KM means the walk(s) may vary in length from 3km to 10km.

BIKES indicates the walk has a path which is suitable for ordinary bikes. *XBIKES* means the walk is not suitable for, or does not permit, cycling. *MTBIKES* means the track is suitable for mountain or all-terrain bikes.

CIRC means the walk can be circular, while *XCIRC* shows the walk is not circular and you must return more or less the way you came.

The *1-A-1* Code:
The first number (*1*, *2* or *3*) indicates how easy the walk is.
1 the walk is easy.
2 the walk is of medium difficulty, eg standard hillwalking, not dangerous nor requiring special knowledge or equipment.
3 is difficult: care and preparation and a map are needed.

A, *B* or *C* indicate how easy it is to find the path.
A the route is easy to find. The way is either marked or otherwise obvious.
B the route is not very obvious, but you'll get there.
C you will need a map and preparation or a guide.

The last number (*1*, *2* or *3*) indicates what to wear on your feet.
1 ordinary outdoor shoes, including trainers, are probably okay unless the ground is very wet.
2 you will need walking boots.
3 you will need serious walking or hiking boots.

The *1-A-1* code is employed both for a designated walk and wherever there is more than a short stroll required to get to somewhere, eg a waterfall or a monument.

Part 1

Scotland the best

Wha's Like Us?

Helmsdale

The wee town on the A9 between Inverness and Wick that you might hurtle through. We should stop more often! Though not an old town, built in the 1880s, it charmingly and subtly reveals the ancient spirit and recent history of this northern coast and the strath behind it.

For a small place, it's well served for accommodation and food, with everything in the main street. The Telford Bridge and the sentinel church (with chiming bells) are lit at night and there are great walks along the river and the coast. It deserves our attention and anywhere with the Bohemian Bar on one corner and the Bannockburn Bar on the other has got to be interesting.

Knapdale

Hardly anyone knows where Knapdale is – it seems like it should be in the Lake District. But it's the north bit of the Kintyre peninsula and its location, amidst the most serrated of Scotland's coastline with islands large and small visible from innumerable perspectives, means that from close up and afar it is immensely scenic, possibly the most pleasing place to the eye on the western seaboard.

The single-track road, the B8024 that follows the coast from Tarbert to Lochgilphead, skirts and best encapsulates Knapdale. 3km south towards Tarbert, a sign 'To the Coves' takes you 500m to the Kilberry Coves to watch otters and to swim in summer.

The vital feature of Knapdale is its woodland. Thousands of acres of original, diverse, deciduous woodland – oak, birch, hazel and alder and the wildlife that lives there: owls, red squirrels, eagles and hedgerows and wild flower meadows. These forests once clothed Scotland. In Knapdale we rediscover our roots and branches.

Loch Awe

Overshadowed by the bigger lochs, Lomond, Ness and Tay and by those we personally love, Loch Awe has somehow gone unloved. I felt so until one brilliant summer evening in 2009 when, roof of the car open, I drove over from Inveraray to meet the south Loch Awe road in Caledonian forest of oaks and birch, the loch glittering, Ben Cruachan above, and I realised how resplendent is this mighty body of water that stabs right through the heart of Argyll.

A quick evaluation shows how many exceptional places are associated with it: the plethora of woodland walks, fishing, cycling and picnicking as well as churches, a ruined castle and first-rate hotels. From these perspectives and countless places on the south loch road, it becomes clear that Loch Awe is actually quite awesome.

Pool House at Poolewe

No apologies for a personal paean to this labour of love. This is a historic house and its transformation has been a remarkable venture for the Harrison Family who've been working to realise their vision for years. Its situation at the lochhead made it a wartime operations base and it has a special place in naval history. Rooms are named after ships and one is themed on the *Titanic*, whose captain was related to mum Margaret Harrison's grandfather.

All the rooms are presented with extraordinary attention to detail. The family works to create the garden which provides herbs and salad stuff and in 2010 they're creating a new Chinese suite to complement the Indian one they have already (with maharajah bed and palatial bathroom; surely the most sumptuous single room in the land).

The whole homely yet exotic experience is outrageously inexpensive. Go love this place as much as they do.

The Border Lands

I'm a Borders lad and like most people I'm easily drawn back to my roots. My home town of Jedburgh is the first town in Scotland, and is picturesque and peaceful. Most visitors trundle past on the A68 as they do with most of the Border towns on the way to or from Edinburgh.

This is a pity! There is much to see in the Border lands. Melrose is much admired and is the Borders' Food Town but there are many other villages and towns that invite exploration in the gentle green hills: Lilliesleaf, Bowden, Denholm, Newtown St Boswells and Kelso with its abbey and a couple of good places to eat. Hawick also has a great deli/café and an intrepid tearoom.

But the best way to appreciate the Borders is to wander in it and its bucolic serenity – as soothing an antidote to the stresses of life as you can get for almost nothing.

Scotland's population has never been much over 5 million and yet we discovered, invented or manufactured for the first time the following quite important things.

The Advertising Film
Anaesthesia
Ante-Natal Clinics
Antiseptics
Artificial Ice
The Alpha Chip
The ATM
The Bank of England
The Bicycle
Bovril
The Bowling Green
The Bus
Colour Photographs
The Compass
The Decimal Point
The Documentary
Dolly, the Cloned Sheep
Electric Light
Encyclopaedia Britannica
The Fax Machine
Fingerprinting
The Flushing Toilet
The Fountain Pen
Gardenias
The Gas Mask
Geology
Golf Clubs
The Golf Course
Helium
The Hypodermic Syringe
Insulin
Interferon
The Kaleidoscope
Kinetic Energy

The Lawnmower
Life Insurance
The Locomotive
Logarithms
The Mackintosh
Marmalade
Motor Insurance
The Modern Road Surface
Morphine
Neon
The Overdraft
Paraffin
Penicillin
The Photocopier
The Pneumatic Tyre
Postage Stamps
Postcards
Radar
The Steam Engine
Street Lighting
Stocks and Shares
The Telegraph
The Telephone
Television
Tennis Courts
The Thermometer
The Threshing Machine
Typhoid Vaccine
The Theory of Combustion
The Vacuum Flask
Video
Wave Power
Writing Paper

and *Auld Lang Syne*

Part 2

Scot
land
the
best

Historical
Places

Linlithgow Palace

*Centre of
Linlithgow*

HS

From the Great Hall, built for James I,
King of Scots, with its huge adjacent
kitchens, and the North Range with loch
views, you get a real impression of the
lavish lifestyle of the Scottish court. Not
as busy as some HS attractions but it is
fabulous. King's Fountain restoration
has added to the palace appeal.

Caerlaverock

*17km south of
Dumfries by B725*

HS

Fairy-tale fortress within double moat
and manicured lawns, the daunting
frontage being the apex of an unusual
triangular shape. Since 1270, the bastion
of the Maxwells, the Wardens of the
West Marches. Destroyed by Bruce,
besieged in 1640. The whole castle
experience is here. Kids' adventure park.

Dunnottar Castle

*3km south of
Stonehaven on
the coast road
just off A92*

Like Slains further north, these ruins are
impressively and precariously perched
on a cliff top. Historical links with
Wallace, Mary, Queen of Scots (the odd
night) and even Oliver Cromwell, whose
Roundheads besieged it in 1650. Mel
Gibson's *Hamlet* was filmed here (bet
you don't remember the film) and the
Honours of Scotland (the Scots crown
jewels) were once held here. 400m walk
from car park or walk along the cliff top
from Stonehaven.

Castle Tioram

*5km from A861
just north of
Acharacle*

ATMOS

A romantic ruin where you don't need
the saga to sense the place, and maybe
the mystery is better than the history.
Park on the serenely beautiful shoreline
then walk across a short causeway.
Pronounced 'Cheerum'. Musical beach
at nearby Kentra Bay.

Elgin Cathedral

Centre of Elgin
HS

Set in a tranquil meadow by the river, the scattered ruins and surrounding graveyard of what was once Scotland's finest cathedral. The nasty Wolf of Badenoch burned it down in 1390, but there are 13th century and medieval renewals. The octagonal chapterhouse is especially revered, but this is an impressive and evocative slice of history. HS have made great job of recent restorations. Now the tower can be climbed.

Kildrummy Castle

15km southwest of Alford on A97
HS
ATMOS

The most complete 13th-century castle in Scotland, an HQ for the Jacobite uprising of 1715 and an evocative and very Highland site. Here the invitation in the old HS advertising to 'bring your imagination' is truly valid.

Kisimull Castle

Isle of Barra
HS

Atmospheric medieval fortress home of the MacNeils that sits on a rocky outcrop in the bay. Built in the 11th century, burnt in the 18th and restored by the 45th chief, an American architect, but was unfinished when he died in 1970. An essential pilgrimage for all MacNeils, it is fascinating for the rest of us, a grim exterior belying an unusual internal layout: a courtyard that seems unchanged and rooms betwixt renovation and decay.

Edzell Castle

3km off Edzell main street; signed
HS

Pleasing red sandstone ruin in bucolic setting – birds twitter, rabbits run. The notable walled parterre Renaissance garden created by Sir David Lindsay way back in 1604 is the oldest-preserved in Scotland. The wall niches are nice. Lotsa lobelias! Mary, Queen of Scots was here (she so got around).

Bothwell Castle

15km southeast of Glasgow near M74 junction 5
HS

Hugely impressive 13th-century ruin, the home of the Black Douglas, overlooking Clyde (with fine walks). Remarkable considering its proximity to the city that there is hardly any 21st-century intrusion except yourself. Pay to go inside or just sit and watch the Clyde go by.

Fort George

18km northeast of Inverness via A96 by Ardersier
HS

A vast site and 'one of the most outstanding artillery fortifications in Europe'. Planned after Culloden as a base for George II's army and completed 1769, it has remained unaltered ever since and allows a very complete picture. May provoke palpitations in the Nationalist heart, but it's heaven for militarists and altogether impressive (don't miss the museum). It's hardly a ruin of course, and is still occupied by the Army.

Dunollie Castle

Just outside Oban via Corran Esplanade towards Ganavan

Bit of a scramble up and a slither down (and the run itself is not 'safe'), but views are superb. More atmospheric than Dunstaffnage and not commercialised. You can climb one flight up, but the ruin is only a remnant of the great stronghold of the Lorn Kings that it was. The Macdougals, who took it over in the 12th century, still live in the house below.

Tarbert Castle

Tarbert, Argyll Steps up from Harbour Road

Strategically and dramatically overlooking the sheltered harbour of this epitome of a West Highland port. Unsafe to clamber over, it's for the timeless view rather than an evocation of tangible history that it's worth finding the way up.

Kilchurn Castle

Loch Awe
HS

The romantic ruin at the head of awesome Loch Awe. A very pleasant spot for loch reflections; and others.

St Andrews Cathedral

St Andrews
HS

The ruins of the largest church in Scotland before the Reformation, a place of great influence and pilgrimage. St Rule's Tower and the jagged fragment of the huge West Front in their striking position at the convergence of the main streets and overlooking the sea, are remnants of its great glory.

Crichton Castle

Pathhead, 28km south of Edinburgh
HS

Massive Border keep dominating the Tyne valley in pristine countryside. The 15th-century collegiate church is nearby. Good picnic spots below by the river though may be overgrown in summer.

Tantallon Castle

5km east of North Berwick
HS

Dramatic cliff top setting with views to Bass Rock. Dates from 1350 with massive 'curtain wall' to see it through stormy weather and stormy history. The Red Douglases and their friends kept the world at bay.

Ruthven Barracks

2km from Kingussiek
HS

Visible from A9 especially at night when it's illuminated, these former barracks built by the English Redcoats as part of the campaign to tame the Highlands after the first Jacobite rising in 1715, were actually destroyed by the Jacobites in 1746 after Culloden. It was here that Bonnie Prince Charlie sent his final order, 'Let every man seek his own safety', signalling the absolute end of the doomed cause. Life for the soldiers is well described and visualised.

Haddo House

✓ ✓

Tarves, by Ellon
NTS

Designed by William Adam for the Earl of Aberdeen, the Palladian-style mansion itself a bit less accessible after NTS cuts but the serenely superb grounds open always. Not so much a house, more a leisure land in the best possible taste, with bluebells, wild garlic and autumn trees, a pleasant café, estate shop and gentle education. Grand house, full of things; the basements are the places to ponder. Glorious window by Burne-Jones in the chapel. Occasional afternoon teas followed by evening service – heaven (May-Oct)! Limited programme of other events. House: guided tours (must book) 0844 493 2179. Gardens all year till sunset.

Mount Stuart

✓ ✓

Bute
ATMOS

Unique Victorian Gothic house; echoes 3rd Marquis of Bute's passion for mythology, astronomy, astrology and religion. Amazing splendour, yet the atmosphere is intimate and romantic. Italian antiques, notable paintings, fascinating attention to detail with surprise humorous touches. Equally grand gardens with fabulous walks, sea views. Stylish visitor centre with restaurant/ coffee shop and well-curated gallery space (and in woods). Even the garden centre is tasteful.

Manderston

✓ ✓

Duns
ATMOS

The swan-song of the Great Classical House, one of the UK's finest examples of Edwardian opulence. *The* Edwardian CH of TV fame. The family still live there. Below stairs as fascinating as up (the silver staircase!); sublime gardens (don't miss the woodland garden on other side of the lake, or the marble dairy).

Traquair

Innerleithen, 2km from A72

An archetypal romantic Border retreat that is steeped in Jacobite history (ask about the Bear gates). Human proportions, liveability and lots of atmosphere. An enchanting house, a maze (20th century) and a tranquil duck pond in the garden. Traquair ale is still brewed. 1745 cottage tearoom, pottery and candle-making. Traquair has a cool events programme including fairs in May and usually in Aug. Woodland walks.

Newhailes

Musselburgh

NTS

Well signed from the Portobello end of Musselburgh (3km). NTS flagship time-capsule project stabilising the microcosm of 18th-century history encapsulated here and uniquely intact. With great rococo interiors, this is very liveable, especially the library. A rural sanctuary near the city: parklands, shell grotto, summer house. Tours last 1 hour 15 minutes.

Dumfries House

Near Cumnock and Auchinleck

HS

One of the finest Palladian mansions in the country, Dumfries House was saved for the nation in '07 by a consortium led by the Prince of Wales (and with £5M from the Scottish Government). The 750 acres of grounds and 18th-century apartments with their priceless Chippendale furniture and pristine artefacts are to open to the public by appointment but you can drop in, so check first. Café.

Paxton

✓

Near Berwick

Off the B6461 to Swinton and Kelso, 6km from A1. A country park and Adam mansion with Chippendales and Trotters; the picture gallery is a National

Gallery outstation. They've made a very good job of the wallpapering. 80 acres of woodlands to walk. Good adventure playground. Restored Victorian boathouse and salmon fishing museum on the Tweed. Red-squirrel hide. Evening music programme in Jul; other events. Tours.

Gosford House

Near Aberlady

On the A198 between Longniddry and Aberlady, Gosford estate is behind a high wall and oddly stunted vegetation. Imposing house with centre block by Robert Adam and the wing you visit by William Young who did Glasgow City Chambers. The Marble Hall houses the remarkable collections of the unbroken line of Earls of Wemyss. Priceless art, informally displayed. Superb grounds.

Floors Castle

Kelso

More vast mansion than old castle, the ancestral home of the Duke of Roxburghe overlooks with imposing grandeur the town and the Tweed. 18th-century with later additions. You're led round lofty public rooms past family collections of fine furniture, tapestries and porcelain. Priceless; spectacularly impractical. Good garden centre and excellent tearoom, The Terrace; café also on courtyard by the house.

Mellerstain

Near Gordon/Kelso

Home of the Earl of Haddington. One of Scotland's great Georgian houses, begun in 1725 by William Adam and completed by Robert. Outstanding decorative interiors (the ceilings are *sans pareil*) especially the library and spectacular exterior. Courtyard teahouse and beautiful gardens.

Thirlestane

Lauder

A castellate/baronial seat of the Earls and Duke of Lauderdale and family home of the Maitlands. Extraordinary staterooms, especially plaster work; once again the ceilings must be seen to be believed. The nurseries (with toy collection), the kitchens and the laundry are more approachable. Complex opening times.

Fyvie

Fyvie, 40km northwest of Aberdeen
NTS
☕

Fyvie is an important stop on the 'Castle Trail' which links the great houses of Aberdeenshire. Before opulence fatigue sets in, see this pleasant baronial pile first (thee are 13 rooms on show). It was lived in until the 1980s so it feels less remote than most. Fantastic roofscape and ceilings. The *best* tearoom. Tree-lined acres; loch side walks. Complex opening hours. Grounds are open all year.

Crathes

Near Banchory, 25km west of Aberdeen
NTS
☕

In superb gardens, a 'fairy-tale castle': a tower house which is actually interesting to visit. Up and down spiral staircases and into small but liveable rooms. The notable painted ceilings and the Long Gallery at the top are all worth lingering over. 350 years of the Burnett family are ingrained in this oak. A big event programme ranges from concerts to craft fairs. Grounds open all year. Tearoom.

Culloden

Inverness
NTS
ATMOS

Signed from A9 and A96 into Inverness and about 8km from town. The new, state-of-the-art visitor centre puts you in the picture, then there's a 10-minute 'rooftop walk' with perspective or a 40-minute through-the-battlefield walk. Positions of the clans and the troops marked out across the moor; flags enable you to get a real sense of scale. If you go in spring you see how wet and miserable the moor can be (the battle took place on 16 April 1746). No matter how many other folk are there wandering down the lines, a visit to this most infamous of battlefields can still leave a pain in the heart. Centre 9am-6pm (winter 11am-4pm). Ground open at all times for more personal Cullodens.

Battle Of The Braes

10km from Portree, Isle of Skye

Take the main A850 road south for 3km then left, marked 'Braes' for 7km. Monument is on a rise on right. The last battle fought on British soil and a significant place in Scots history. When the Clearances, uninterrupted by any organised opposition, were virtually complete and vast tracts of Scotland had been depopulated for sheep, the Skye crofters finally stood up in 1882 to the Government troops and said enough is enough. A cairn has been erected near the spot where they fought on behalf of 'all the crofters of Gaeldom', a battle which led eventually to the Crofters Act which has guaranteed their rights ever since. At the end of this road at Peinchorran, there are fine views of Raasay (which was devastated by clearances) and Glamaig, the conical Cuillin, across Loch Sligachan.

Glencoe

Glencoe

Not much of a battle, of course, but one of the most infamous massacres in British history. Much has been written (John Prebble's *Glencoe* and others) and a discreetly located visitor centre provides audiovisual scenario. Macdonald monument near Glencoe village and the walk to the more evocative Signal Rock where the bonfire was lit, now a happy woodland trail in this doom-laden landscape. Many other great walks.

Scapa Flow

Orkney Mainland and Hoy

Scapa Flow, surrounded by various of the southern Orkney islands, is one of the most sheltered anchorages in Europe. Hence the huge presence in Orkney of ships and personnel during both wars. The Germans scuttled 54 of their warships here in 1919 and many still lie in the bay. The *Royal Oak* was torpedoed in 1939 with the loss of 833 men. Much still remains of the war years (especially if you're a diver): the rusting hulks, the shore fortifications, the Churchill Barriers and the ghosts of a long-gone army at Scapa and Lyness on Hoy. Evocative visitor centre and naval cemetery at Lyness.

Lilliard's Edge

South of St Boswells

The marvellous hill-top view attests to this strategic location. A cairn marks the grave of Lilliard who, in 1545, joined the Battle of Ancrum Moor against the English 'loons' under the Earl of Angus. 'And when her legs were cuttit off, she fought upon her stumps'. An ancient poem etched on the stone records her legendary... feet.

Killiecrankie

Near Pitlochry
NTS

The first battle of the Jacobite Risings where, in July 1689, the Highlanders lost their leader Viscount (aka Bonnie) Dundee, but won the battle, using the narrow Pass of Killiecrankie. One escaping soldier made a famous leap. Well-depicted scenario in visitor centre; short walk to 'The Leap'. Battle viewpoint and cairn is further along road to Blair Atholl, turning right and doubling back near the Garry Guesthouse and on, almost to A9 underpass (3km from visitor centre). You get the lie of the land from here. Many good walks.

Bannockburn

4km from Stirling near M9 junction 9
NTS

Some visitors might be perplexed as to why 24 June 1314 was such a big deal for the Scots and, apart from the 50m walk to the flag-pole and the huge statue, there's not a lot doing. But the battle against the English did finally secure the place of Robert I (the Bruce) as King of Scots, paving the way for the final settlement with England 15 years later. The Heritage Centre does bring to life the scale of the battle, the horror and the glory. The battlefield itself is thought to lie around the orange building of the high school some distance away, and the best place to see the famous wee burn is from below the magnificent Telford Bridge. Ask at the centre (5km by road). The NTS arrange mega re-enactments in mid September. Controversies still rage among scholars: eg did the English really scarper after only an hour?

Inchmahome Priory

Port of Menteith
HS

The priory ruins on the island in Scotland's only lake, where the infant queen spent her early years cared for by Augustinian monks. Short boat journey from quay near lake hotel. Signal the ferryman by turning the board to the island, much as she did.

Mary, Queen of Scots' House

Jedburgh

Historians quibble but this long-standing museum claims to be 'the' house where she fell ill in 1566 but still made it over to visit the injured Bothwell at Hermitage Castle 50km away. Tower house in good condition; displays and well-told saga.

Loch Leven Castle

Near Kinross
HS

The ultimate in romantic penitentiaries; on the island in the middle of the loch, clearly visible from the M90. Not much left of the ruin to fill out the fantasy, but this is where Mary spent 10 months in 1568 before her famous escape and her final attempt to get back the throne.

Dundrennan Abbey

Near Auchencairn
HS

Mary got around and there are innumerable places where she spent the night. This was where she spent her last one on Scottish soil, leaving next day from Port Mary (nothing to see there but a beach, 2km along the road skirting the sinister MoD range, the pier long gone). The Cistercian abbey (established 1142) which harboured her on her last night is now a tranquil ruin.

Lennoxlove House

Near Haddington

Houses her 'death mask'; it does seem small for someone who was supposedly 6 feet tall!

Prince Charlie's Bay or Strand

Eriskay

The uncelebrated, unmarked and quietly beautiful beach where Charlie first landed in Scotland to begin the 1745 Jacobite Rebellion. Nothing much has changed (except the pier for Barra ferry is adjacent) and this crescent of sand with soft machair and a turquoise sea is still a special place.

Loch Nan Uamh, The Prince's Cairn

7km from Lochailort, near Arisaig
ATMOS

This is the traditional spot (pronounced 'Loch Na Nuan') where Charlie embarked for France in September 1746, having lost the battle and the cause. The rocky headland also overlooks the bay and skerries where he'd landed in July the year before to begin the campaign. This place was the beginning and the end and it has all the romance necessary to be utterly convincing. Is that a French ship out there in the mist?

Glenfinnan

Glenfinnan
NTS

Here he raised his standard to rally clans to the Jacobite cause. For a while on that day in August 1745 it looked as if few would come. Then pipes were heard and 600 Camerons came marching from the valley (where the viaduct now spans). That must have been one helluva moment. There is a powerful sense of place and history here. The visitor centre has a good map of Charlie's path through Scotland – somehow he touched all the most alluring places! Climb the tower or take the long view from Loch Shiel.

Culloden

Inverness
NTS
ATMOS

The infamous battlefield where the Jacobite cause died on 16 April 1746, leaving the prince a defeated fugitive.

Bruce's Stone

*Glen Trool near
Newton Stewart*

The stone, in Galloway Forest Park, is signed and marks the area where Bruce's guerrilla band rained boulders onto the pursuing English in 1307 after routing the main army at Solway Moss.

Bannockburn

*4km from Stirling
near M9
junction 9*
NTS

The climactic battle in 1314, when Bruce decisively whipped the English and secured the kingdom. The scale of the battle can be visualised at the heritage centre but not so readily in the field.

Arbroath Abbey

Arbroath
HS

Signing place of the famous Declaration of the Scots nobility, united behind the king, to gain international recognition of the independence they had won on the battlefield. What it says is stirring stuff; the original is in Edinburgh. Great interpretation centre.

Dunfermline Abbey Church

Dunfermline
HS

Here, some tangible evidence: Bruce's tomb. Buried in 1329, his remains were discovered wrapped in gold cloth when the site was being cleared for the new church in 1818. Other great kings also buried here were not so identifiable (Bruce's ribcage had been cut to remove his heart). With great national emotion he was reinterred under the pulpit. Look up and see Robert carved on the skyline.

Melrose Abbey

Melrose
HS

Bruce asked that his heart be buried here after it was taken to the Crusades to aid the army in their battles. A contemporary lead casket thought to contain it was excavated from the chapter house; it was reburied and is marked with a stone. Let's believe in this!

The Lost Valley

Glencoe
2-B-2
ATMOS

The secret glen where the ill-fated Macdonalds hid the cattle they'd stolen from the Lowlands and which became (with politics and power struggles) their undoing. A narrow, wooded cleft takes you between the imposing and gnarled '3 Sisters' Hills and over the threshold (God knows how the cattle got there) into the huge bowl of Coire Gabhail. The place envelops you in its tragic history, more redolent perhaps than any of the massacre sites. Park on the A82 6.5km from the visitor centre 300m west of the white bungalow by the road (always cars parked here). Follow clear path down to and across the River Coe. Ascend keeping burn to left; 1.5km further up, it's best to ford it. Allow 3 hours.

The Whaligoe Steps

Ulbster, 10km
south of Wick

Remarkable structure hewn into sheer cliffs, 365 steps down to a grassy platform – the Bink – and an old fishing station. From 1792, creels of cod, haddock and ling were hauled up these steps for the merchants of Wick and Lybster. Consider these labours as you follow their footsteps in this wild and enchanting place. No rails and can be slippy. Take great care!

Under Edinburgh Old Town

Mary King's Close
under the Royal
Mile
The Vaults under
South Bridge

Mary King's Close, a medieval street closed in 1753; and the Vaults built in the 18th century and sealed up around the time of the Napoleonic Wars. History underfoot for unsuspecting tourists and locals alike. Glimpses of a rather smelly subterranean life way back then. It's dark during the day, and you wouldn't want to get locked in.

The Yesnaby Stacks

*Near Skara Brae,
Orkney Mainland*

A cliff top viewpoint that's so wild, so dramatic and, if you walk near the edge, so precarious that its supernaturalism verges on the uneasy. Shells of wartime lookout posts echo the melancholy spirit of the place. It's about 30km from Kirkwall and way out west. Follow directions from Marwick Head.

The Fairy Glen

Skye
ATMOS

A place so strange, it's hard to believe that it's merely a geological phenomenon. Entering Uig on the A855 (becomes A87) from Portree, there's a turret on the left (Macrae's Folly). Take road on right marked Balnaknock for 2km and you enter an area of extraordinary conical hills which, in certain conditions of light and weather, seems to entirely justify its legendary provenance. Your mood may determine whether you believe they were good or bad fairies, but there's supposed to be an incredible 365 of these grassy hillocks, some 35m high – well, how else could they be here?

Clava Cairns

*Near Culloden,
Inverness*

Near Culloden, these curious chambered cairns stand in a grove of trees near a river in the middle of 21st-century nowhere. This spot can make you feel either a glow or goosepimples.

The Clootie Well

*Between Tore on
the A9 and Avoch*
ATMOS

This spooky place is easily missed (though there is a marked car park on the right side of the road going east). What you see is hundreds of rags or clouts: pieces of clothing hanging on tree branches around the spout of an ancient well where the wearer might be healed. They stretch up the hill behind and though some may have been here a long time, the place seems to have been commodified like everywhere else so there's plenty of new socks and t-shirts with messages. It is all fairly weird.

Burn o' Vat

Near Ballater

This impressive, rather spooky glacial curiosity on Royal Deeside is a popular spot and well worth the short walk. 8km from Ballater towards Aberdeen on main A93, take B9119 for Huntly for 2km to the car park at the Muir of Dinnet nature reserve. Some scrambling to reach the huge 'pot' from which the burn flows to Loch Kinord. SNH visitor centre. 1.1km circular walk to vat, 7km to loch. Can be busy on fine weekends, odd when you find it deserted.

Crichope Linn

Near Thornhill
ATMOS

A supernatural sliver of glen inhabited by water spirits of various tempera- ments (and midges). Take road for Cample on A76 Dumfries to Kilmarnock road just south of Thornhill; at village (2km) there's a wooden sign so take left for 2km. Discreet sign and gate on right is easy to miss, but park in quarry 100m further on. Take care: can be wet and very slippy. Gorge is a 10-minute schlep from the gate. We saw red squirrels!

Hell's Lum Cave

Near Gardenstown, Moray

Off the B9031 signed for Cullykhan Bay. From car park (200m from main road), you walk down to bay and can see on left a scar on the hill which marks the 'lum', approached along the shoreline. Lots of local mythology surrounds this wild and beautiful spot. In the cave itself you hear what sounds like children crying.

Part 3

Scotland the best

Strolls, Walks & Hikes

Popular and notable hills in the various regions of Scotland but not including Munros or difficult climbs. Always best to remember that the weather can change very quickly. Take an OS map on higher tops. See p. 7 for walk codes.
The 6 Trossachs hills are listed in their own section on p. 33.

Suilven

✓ ✓

Lochinver
731m
2-C-3
Allow 8 hours return

From close or far away, this is one of Scotland's most awe-inspiring mountains. The 'sugar loaf' can seem almost insurmountable, but in good weather it's not so difficult. Route from Inverkirkaig 5km south of Lochinver on road to Achiltibuie, turns up track by Achin's Bookshop on the path for the Kirkaig Falls; once at the loch, you head for the Bealach, the central waistline through an unexpected dyke and follow track to the top. The slightly quicker route from the north (Glencanisp) following a stalkers' track that eventually leads to Elphin, also heads for the central breach in the mountain's defences. Either way it's a long walk in; 8km before the climb. At the top, the most enjoyable 100m in the land and below – amazing Assynt. Take OS map.

Stac Pollaidh/Polly

✓ ✓

Near Ullapool
613m
2-B-3
Allow 3–4 hours return

This hill described variously as 'perfect', 'preposterous' and 'great fun'; it certainly has character and, rising out of the Sutherland moors on the road to Achiltibuie off the A835 north from Ullapool, demands to be climbed. The route everyone takes is from the car park by Loch Lurgainn 8km from the main road. The new path takes you (either way) round the hill and up from the north side. The path to the pinnacles is exposed and can be off-putting. Best half-day hill climb in the North.

Quinag

Near Lochinver
Allow 5 hours
return

Like Stac Polly (p. 31), this Corbett (pronounced 'Koonyag') has amazing presence and seems more formidable than it
actually is. Park off the A894 to Kylesku.
An up-and-down route can take in 6 or
7 tops in your 5-hour expedition (or cur-
tail). Once again, awesome Assynt!

Goat Fell

Arran
874m
2-B-2
Allow 4 hours
return
NTS

Starting from the car park at Cladach
before Brodick Castle grounds 3km from
town, or from Corrieburn Bridge south
of Corrie further up the coast (12km). A
worn path, a steady climb, rarely much
of a scramble but a rewarding afternoon's exertion. Some scree and some
view! Usually not a circular route.

The Cobbler (aka Ben Arthur)

Arrochar
881m
2-B-3

Perennial favourite of the Glasgow hill-
walker and, for sheer exhilaration, the
most popular of 'the Arrochar Alps'. A
motorway path ascends from the A83
on the other side of Loch Long from
Arrochar (park in laybys near Succoth
road end; there are always loads of cars)
and takes 2.5-3 hours to traverse the up
'n' down route to the top. Just short of a
Munro at 881m, it has 3 tops of which
the north peak is the simplest scramble
(central and south peaks for climbers).
Where the way is not marked, consult.

Dunadd

Kilmartin, north
of Lochgilphead
2-B-2
HS

Halfway from Kilmartin on A816. Less of
a hill, more of a lump, but it's where
they crowned the kings of Dalriada for
half a millennium. Rocky staircases and
soft, grassy top. Stand there when the
Atlantic rain sheets in and... you get wet
like even kings did. Or when the light is
good you can see the glen and coast.

Ben Venue & Ben A'An

*15km west of
Callander
Ben Venue: 727m
Allow 4-5 hours
return
Ben A'An: 415m
Allow 2-3 hours
2-B-3*

Two strenuous but not difficult tops with superb views. Ben Venue is the more serious. Start from Kinlochard side at Ledard or more usually from Loch Katrine corner before Loch Achray Hotel (waymarked from new car park). Ben A'an starts with a steep climb from the main A821 near the same corner along from the Tigh Mor mansions (just before the corner). Scramble at the top.

Benn Shian

*Strathyre
600m
2-B-3
Allow 3 hours
return*

A Trossachs favourite; not taxing. From the village main road (the A74 to Lochearnhead), cross bridge opposite Monro Inn, turn left after 200m then a path to right at 50m; a steep start through woods. Overlooking the village and with views to Crianlarich and Ben Vorlich.

Doon Hill

*The Faerie Knowe,
Aberfoyle
1-B-1
Allow 1 hour*

Legendary hillock. Tree at top is home of the 'People of Quietness'. Go round it 7 times and your wish will be granted, but go round backwards at your peril. From main street take Manse Rd by garden centre. 1km past cemetery; signed.

Ben Vorlich

*2-B-3
Allow 5 hours
return*

Also approached from south Lochearn road; from Ardvorlich House 5km from A84. Enter 'East Gate' and follow signs for Glen Vorlich. The track splits after 1.5km, take right then southeast side to come to north ridge of mountain.

Ben Ledi

*Near Callander
2-B-3
Allow 4 hours*

The Trossachs spread before you as you climb this Corbett. West from town on A84 through Pass of Leny. First left over bridge to car park. Well-trod path, ridge at top. Return by Stank Glen; follow river.

Criffel

*New Abbey, near
Dumfries*
569m
2-A-2

12km south by A710 to New Abbey, which Criffel dominates. It's only 569m, but seems higher. From the top there are exceptional views as far as the English lakes and across to the Borders. It's a granite lump with brilliant outcrops of quartzite. The annual race gets up and back to the Abbey Arms in under an hour; you can take it easier. Start 3km south of village, turnoff A710 100m from one of the curious painted bus shelters signed for Ardwell Mains Farm. Park before the farm buildings and get on up.

Merrick

*Near Newton
Stewart*
843m
2-B-3
Allow 4 hours

Go from bonnie Glen Trool via Bargrennan 14km north on the A714. Bruce's Stone (marking the spot where Robert I's men ambushed an English force in 1307) is there at the start. The highest peak in Southern Scotland, it's a strenuous though straightforward climb, a grassy ridge to the summit and glorious scenery.

North Berwick Law & Traprain Law

*East Lothian
Both 1-A-1*

North Berwick Law is a conical volcanic hill and a beacon in the East Lothian landscape. Traprain Law nearby is higher, easy and celebrated by rock climbers, but it also has major prehistoric significance as a hill fort citadel of the Goddodin and has a definite aura. North Berwick Law is also simple and rewarding – leave town by Law Rd; the path is marked beyond the houses. Car park and picnic site. Views 'to the Cairngorms' (!) and along the Forth. There's a famous whalebone at the top.

Ruberslaw

*Denholm, near
Hawick*
424m
2-A-2

Smooth hummock above the Teviot val-ley affords views of 7 counties, including Northumberland. Millennium plaque on top. It's a gentle climb taking about 1 hour from the usual start at Denholm Hill Farm (private land; and be aware of the livestock). Leave Denholm at corner of green by post office and go past war memorial. Take left after 2km to farm.

Tinto Hill

*Near Biggar and
Lanark*
707m
2-A-2
Allow 2 hours

A favourite climb in South/Central Scotland with easy access to the start from Fallburn on A73 near Symington, 10km south of Lanark. Park 100m behind Tinto Hills farm shop. Good, simple track there and back though it has its ups and downs before you get there. Braw views. Allow 2 hours though annual racers do it in under 30 minutes.

Dumgoyne

Near Blanefield
2-A-2
Allow 3-4 hours

Close to Glasgow and almost a moun-tain, so a popular non-strenuous hike. Huge presence, sits above A81 and Glengoyne Distillery (open to public). Approach from Strathblane war memo-rial via Campsie Dene road. 7km track (or take the steep way up from the distillery). Take care on outcrops.

Conic Hill

*Balmaha,
Loch Lomond*
358m
2-A-2
1.5 hours up

One of the first Highland hills you reach from Glasgow. Stunning views also of Loch Lomond and the Ben. Ascend through woodland from the corner of Balmaha (the visitor centre) car park. Watch for buzzards and your footing on the final crumbly bits. Access all year with new Access Code. Easy walks also on the nearby island, Inchcailloch.

Kinnoull Hill

Perth
1-A-1

Various starts from town (the path from beyond Branklyn Garden on the Dundee Rd is less frequented) to the wooded ridge above the Tay with its tower and incredible views to south from the precipitous cliffs. Surprisingly extensive area of hillside common and it's not difficult to get lost. The leaflet/map from Perth tourist information centre helps. Local lurv spot after dark.

Bennachie

Near Aberdeen
528m
2-B-2
2 hours

The pilgrimage hill, an easy 528m often busy at weekends but never disappoints. Various trails take you to 'the Taps' from 3 main car parks. (1) From the new Bennachie Centre: 3km north of Inverurie on the A96, take left to chapel of Garioch (pronounced 'Geery'), then left (it's signed). Centre closed Mon. (2) 16km north of Inverurie on the A96, take B9002 through Oyne, then signed on left – picnic here among the pines. (3) The Donview car park 5km north of Monymusk towards Blairdaff – the longer, gentler walk in. All car parks have trail-finders. From the fortified top you see what Aberdeenshire is about. Bennachie's soulmate, Tap o' Noth, is 20km west. Easy approach via Rhynie on A97 (then 3km).

Heaval

Barra
1.5 hours return

The mini-Matterhorn that rises above Castlebay is an easy and rewarding climb. At 1250ft, it's steep in places but never over-taxing. You see 'the road to Mingulay'. Start up hill through Castlebay, park behind the new-build house, find path via Our Lady of the Sea.

Scots Pine, with oak and birch etc, formed the great Caledonian Forest which once covered most of Scotland. Native Scots Pine is very different from the regimented rows of pine trees we associate with forestry plantations and which now drape much of the countryside. It is more like a deciduous tree with reddish bark and irregular foliage; no two ever look the same. The remnants of the great stands of pine are beautiful to see, mystical and majestic, a joy to walk among and no less worthy of conservation perhaps than a castle or a bird of prey. Here are some places you will find them.

Rothiemurchus Forest near Aviemore

Glentanar near Ballater

Around **Braemar** and **Grantown-On-Spey**

Around **Linn of Dee**, especially the back road to Mar Lodge

Strathyre South of the village near Callander on right of the main road after Loch Lubnaig

Achray Forest near Aberfoyle

Blackwood of Rannoch south of Loch Rannoch

Rowardennan Loch Lomond

Shores of **Loch Maree**, **Loch Torridon** and around **Loch Clair, Glen Torridon**

Glen Affric near Drumnadrochit

Native pinewoods aren't found south of Perthshire, but there are fine plantation examples in southern Scotland at:

Glentress near Peebles

Shambellie Estate near Dumfries

Ardnamurchan

*Ardnamurchan
Peninsula*

For anyone who loves trees (or hills, coastal scenery and raw nature), this far-flung peninsula is a revelation. Approach from south via Corran ferry on A82 south of Fort William; or north from Lochailort on A830 Mallaig–Fort William road; or from Mull. Many trails. To visit Ardnamurchan is to fall in love with Scotland again and again. Woods especially around Loch Sunart. Good campsite at Resipole and lovely food at Lochaline.

Randolph's Leap

Near Forres
CIRC
XBIKES
1-A-2
1-4km

Spectacular gorge of the little Findhorn lined with beautiful beech woods and a great place to swim or picnic, so listen up. Go either: 10km south of Forres on the A940 for Grantown, then the B9007 for Ferness and Carrbridge. 1km from the sign for Logie Steading and 300m from the narrow stone bridge, there's a pull-over place on the bend. The woods are on the other side of the road. Or: take the A939 south from Nairn or north from Grantown and at Ferness take the B9007 for Forres. Approaching from this direction, it's about 6km along the road; the pull-over is on your right. If you come to Logie Steading in this direction you've missed it; don't – you will miss one of the sylvan secrets of the North.

Lochaweside

Loch Awe
CIRC
XBIKES
2-A-2
2-8km

Unclassified road on north side of loch between Kilchrenan and Ford, centred on Dalavich. Leaflet available locally describes 6 walks in the mixed, mature forest all starting from parking places on the road. 3 starting from the Barnaline car park are trail-marked and could be followed without brochure. Avich Falls route crosses River Avich after 2km with falls on return route. Inverinan Glen is always nice. Timber trail from the Big Tree/Cruachan car park 2km south of Dalavich takes in the loch, waterfall and is easy on the eye and foot (4km). Track from car park north of Kilchrenan on the B845 back to Taynuilt isn't on the leaflet, may be less travelled and also fine.

Puck's Glen

✓

12km north of Dunoon
CIRC   XBIKES
1-A-1
3km

Close to the gates of Younger Botanic Garden at Benmore on the other side of the A815 to Strachur. A short, exhilarating woodland walk from convenient car park. Ascend through trees then down into a fairy glen, follow the burn back to the road. Some swimming pools.

Rothiemurchus Forest

✓

Near Aviemore
1-A-2

The place to experience the magic and majesty of the great Caledonian Forest and the beauty of Scots Pine. Approach from B970, the road that parallels the A9 from Coylumbridge to Kincraig/Kingussie. 2km from Inverdruie near Coylumbridge follow sign for Loch an Eilean; one of the most perfect lochans in these or any woods. Loch circuit 5km. Info, sustenance and shopping at Rothiemurchus visitor centre, Inverdruie with wonderful Ord Ban café/restaurant.

Ariundle Oakwoods

✓

Strontian
CIRC
MTBIKES
1-A-2
5km

35km Fort William via Corran Ferry. Walk brochure at Strontian tourist info centre. Walks around Loch Sunart and Ariundle: oak and other native species. See how different Scotland's landscape was before the Industrial Revolution used up the wood. Start over town bridge, turning right for Polloch. Go on past Ariundle Centre (good home-baking café) and park. 2 walks; well marked.

Inchcailloch Island

Loch Lomond
CIRC
1-A-2
3km

Surprisingly large island near Balmaha, criss-crossed with easy, interesting woodland walks with the loch always there through the trees. A pleasant option is to row from Balmaha Boatyard (£10 a boat at TGP). Also a regular ferry.

Balmacarra

Lochalsh
Woodland Garden
CIRC
XBIKES
1-A-1

5km south Kyle of Lochalsh on A87. A fragrant and verdant amble around the shore of Loch Alsh, centred on Lochalsh House. Mixed woods in formal garden setting: you are confined to paths. Views to Skye. Ranger service.

The Birks o' Aberfeldy

Aberfeldy
CIRC
XBIKES
1-A-2
2 hours

Circular walk through oak, beech and the birch (or birk) woods of the title, easily reached and signed from main street (1km). Steep-sided wooded glen of the Moness Burn with attractive falls, especially the higher one spanned by bridge where the 2 marked walks converge. This is where Burns 'spread the lightsome days' in his eponymous poem.

The Hermitage, Dunkeld

Dunkeld
CIRC
XBIKES
1-A-1

On A9 2km north of Dunkeld. Popular, easy, accessible walks along glen and gorge of River Braan with pavilion overlooking the Falls and further on, Ossian's Cave. Uphill Craig Vinean walks starts here to good viewpoint (2km). Several woody walks around Dunkeld/Birnam. 2km along is Rumbling Bridge, a deep gorge; great spots for swimming beyond.

Glenmore Forest Park

Near Aviemore

Along from Coylumbridge on road to ski resort, the forest-trail area centred on Loch Morlich. Visitor centre has trail maps and an activity programme.

Part 4

Scotland the best

The Islands

Raasay

Regular CalMac ferry from Sconser on Skye

A small car ferry (car useful, but bikes best) from Sconser takes you to this, the best of places. The distinctive flat top of Dun Caan presides over an island whose history and natural history is Highland Scotland in microcosm. The village with rows of mining-type cottages is 3km from jetty. The 'big house', home to the excellent Outdoor Centre, sadly went on fire in '09. Let's hope they rise from the ashes. Views from the lawn, from above the house, or better still from Dun Caan with the Cuillin on one side and Torridon on the other, are exceptional. The island hotel has a bar but could do with some TLC. There's a ruined castle, a secret rhododendron-lined loch for swimming, seals, otters and eagles. Find *Calum's Road* and read the book. Much to explore but go quietly here.

Jura

Regular CalMac ferry from Port Askaig to Feolin Passenger-only ferry from Tayvallich to Craighouse, Easter-Sep.

Jura is remote, scarcely populated and has an ineffable grandeur indifferent to the demands of tourism. Ideal for wild camping, or there's a serviceable hotel and pub in Craighouse. Antlers restaurant is brilliant. Walking guides are essential especially for the Paps, the hills that maintain such a powerful hold over the island. Easiest climb is from Three Arch Bridge; allow 6 hours. In May they run up all of them and back to the distillery in 3 hours. The distillery where The Jura comes from is not beautiful but the drink is; there are tours. Jura House's walled garden is a hidden jewel over the south coastline. Corryvreckan whirlpool is another lure, but you may need a 4-wheel drive to get close enough, and its impressiveness depends upon tides.

Barnhill, Orwell's house where he wrote 1984, isn't open but there are many fascinating side tracks: the wild west coast; around Loch Tarbert; and the long littoral between Craighouse and Lagg. With one road, no street lamps and over 5000 deer, the sound of silence is everything.

Iona

✓ ✓

Regular CalMac ferry from Fionnphort

Strewn with daytrippers – not so much a pilgrimage, more an invasion – but Iona still enchants (as it did the Colourists), especially if you can get away to the Bay at the Back of the Ocean or watch the cavalcade from the hill above the abbey. Or stay: Argyll Hotel is best; St Columba Hotel near the abbey has more rooms and a lovely garden; or B&B. Abbey shop isn't bad. Pilgrimage walks on Tue (10am from St John's Cross). Everything about Iona is benign; even the sun shines here when it's raining on Mull. It is a special place on the planet.

Colonsay

✓ ✓

CalMac ferry from Oban or Islay

Accessible to daytrippers but time ashore is short so you need to arrange accommodation. The island is a haven of wildlife, flowers and beaches and is a serene and popular stopover. 250 metres from the ferry, the refurbished hotel is congenial and convenient. Some holiday cottages and many B&Bs but camping is discouraged. Bar meals and supper at the hotel and 'Pantry' at the pier. A wild 18-hole golf course and bookshop (*sic*) adjacent. Semi-botanical gardens at Colonsay House and fine walks, especially to Oronsay. Don't miss the house at Shell Beach which sells oysters and honey.

Eigg

✓ ✓

CalMac ferry from Mallaig or Arisaig Also Arisaig Marine

After changing hands, much to-do and cause célèbre, the islanders seized the time and Eigg is theirs; and ours. A haven for birds and sealife: otters, eagles and seal colonies. Scot Wildlife Trust warden does weekly walks around the island. Friendly tearoom at pier. Bicycle hire from the shop. Its owner, the irrepressible Sue Kirk, also does B&B, self-catering (near Laig Bay and the singing sands beach) and has a wee restaurant in her house. Great walk to Sgurr an Eigg – an awesome perch on a summer's day. The community also has a great events programme. You can camp.

Rum

✓ ✓

CalMac ferry from Mallaig or via Eigg Murdo Grant's ferry from Arisaig

The large island in the group of Canna, Eigg, Muck and Rum off the coast at Mallaig. Rum the most wild and dramatic has an extraordinary time-warp mansion/museum in Kinloch Castle. Hostel rooms (45 beds) contrast to the antique opulence above and below. Rum is run by Scottish Natural Heritage and there are fine trails, climbs and bird-watching spots. 2 simple walks are marked for the day visitors, but the island reveals its mysteries more slowly. The Doric temple mausoleum to George Bullough, the industrialist whose Highland fantasy the castle was, is a 9km (3-hour) cross-island walk across to Harris Bay. Sighting the sea eagles may be one of the best things that ever happens to you.

St Kilda

✓ ✓

To visit, see www.stkilda.org.uk
NTS

There's nothing quite like St Kilda – anywhere. By far the most remote and removed of the islands here, it is an expedition to get there and one of a physical, cultural and spiritual nature.

Now accorded World Heritage status and run by NTS, it occupies a special place in the heart and soul of the Scots. The NTS ranger's office on St Kilda can be reached on 01870 604628. Sadly I have never been.

Isle Of Tiree

CalMac ferry from Oban or flights from Glasgow

It is an isle, not just an island – it's flat, it has lovely sand and grass and the weather's usually better than the mainland. A bit of wind does keep away the midges. Lots of outdoor activities: famously, windsurfing, but kayaking, birdwatching and other gentle pursuits. The Scarinish Hotel is friendly, local and loved, there are 3 guest houses, a wee hostel and a campsite. Tiree has a unique character different to the islands in this section. But you may long for trees.

Gigha

CalMac ferry from Tayinloan

Romantic small island off the Kintyre coast with classic views of its island neighbours. Easy mainland access (20-minute ferry) contributes to an island atmosphere lacking a feeling of isolation. Like Eigg, Gigha was bought by the islanders so its fragile economy is dependent on your visit. The island is run by a heritage trust. Gardens at Achamore House are a big attraction and its hotel provides comfortable surroundings. Locals are relaxed and friendly. Bike hire. 3 B&Bs including exceptional rooms at the big house and golf (9 holes). Many trails and tracks; ask locally for an information leaflet. Double Beach, where the Queen once swam off the royal yacht; two crescents of sand on either side of the north end of Eilean Garbh isthmus.

Ulva

Ferry from Mull

Off the west coast of Mull. A boat leaves Ulva Ferry on the B8073 26km south of Dervaig. Idyllic wee island with 5 well-marked walks including to the curious basalt columns similar to Staffa, or by causeway to the smaller island of Gometra; plan routes at the Boathouse interpretive centre and tearoom (with Ulva oysters and home-cooked food). 'Sheila's (thatched) Cottage' faithfully restored. No accommodation, though camping can be arranged. A charming Telford church has services 4 times a year. Ulva is a perfect day away from the rat race of downtown Tobermory!

Eriskay

CalMac ferry from Barra

Made famous by the sinking nearby of the SS *Politician* in 1941 and the salvaging of its cargo of whisky, later immortalised by Compton Mackenzie in *Whisky Galore*, this Hebridean gem has all the 'idyllic island' ingredients: perfect beaches, a hill to climb, a pub (called the Politician and telling the story round its walls; it sells decent pub food all day in summer), and the causeway to South Uist (though the road cuts a swathe across the island). Limited B&B and no hotel, but camping is ok if you're dis-creet. Eriskay and Barra together – the pure island experience.

Mingulay

Day trips from Barra
NTS

Deserted mystical island near the south-ern tip of the Outer Hebrides, the sub-ject of one of the definitive island books, *The Road to Mingulay*. Now easily reached in summer by daily trip from Castlebay on Barra: 1.5-hour journey and 3 hours ashore. Last inhabitants left in

1912. Ruined village has the poignant air of St Kilda; similar spectacular cliffs on west side with fantastic rock formations, stacks and a huge natural arch, best viewed from boat. Only birds and sheep live here now.

The Shiants

To visit, check the island website

3 magical, uninhabited tiny islands off east coast of Harris. Read about them in one of the most detailed accounts (a 'love letter') to any small island ever written: *Sea Room* by Adam Nicolson, the guy who owns them. There's a bothy and it's possible to visit by visiting first his website (www.shiantisles.net).

Lismore

CalMac ferry from Oban or Port Appin

Sail from Oban or better from Port Appin 5km off the main A828 Oban-Fort William road, 32km north of Oban; there's a seafood bar/restaurant/hotel to sit and wait. A road runs down the centre of the island (heritage centre and café is a halfway house) but there are many hill and coastal walks; even the near end round Port Ramsay feels away from it all. History, natural history and air. Island bike hire.

Staffa

Trips from Mull, from Iona/Fionnphort or from Oban

For many a must, especially if you're on Mull. The geological phenomenon of Fingal's Cave and Mendelssohn's homage are well known. But it's still impressive. Several boat-trip options, many including the Treshnish Islands.

Part 5

Scot land the best

Outdoor Places

Drumlanrig Castle

7km north of Thornhill
Open Mar-Oct 10am–5pm
House Apr-Aug 11am–4pm

On the A76 near Thornhill in the west Borders in whose romance and history it's steeped, much more than merely a country park; spend a good day, both inside the castle and in the grounds. Apart from *that* art collection (Rembrandt, Holbein and you may remember the Leonardo got stolen, then recovered; it should be back 2010) and the courtyard of shops, the delights include: a great wee tearoom; woodland and riverside walks; an adventure playground; regular events programme, including a farmers' market last Sun of the month (Feb-Oct); and bike hire for explorations along the Nith.

Muirshiel

✓

Near Lochwinnoch

Via Largs (A760) or Glasgow (M8, junction 29 A737 then A760 5km south of Johnstone). North from village on Kilmacolm road for 3km then signed. Muirshiel is the name given to a wider area but the park proper begins 6km on road along the Calder valley. Despite proximity of conurbation, this is a wild and enchanting place for walks, picnics, etc. Trails marked to waterfall and summit views. Extensive events programme. Go look for hen harriers. Escape!

John Muir Country Park

Near Dunbar
ECO

Named after the 19th-century conservationist who founded America's national parks (and the Sierra Club) and who was born in Dunbar (his birthplace is now an interactive museum at 126 High St). This swathe of coastline to the west of the town (known locally as Tyninghame) is an important estuarine nature reserve but is also good for family walks and beachcombing. Can enter via B6370 off A198 to North Berwick or by 'cliff-top' trail from Dunbar or from car park on road into Dunbar from the west at West Barns.

Strathclyde Park

Near Hamilton and Motherwell

15km southeast of Glasgow. Take the M8/A725 interchange or M74 junction 5 or 6. Strathclyde is Scotland's most popular country park, especially for water sports. From canoeing to parascending; you can hire gear here. Also excavated Roman bath house, playgrounds, sports pitches and pleasant walks. Nearby Baron's Haugh and Dalzell Country Park are notable for their nature trails and gardens. However, 'Scotland's Theme Park' fairground and the horrid Alona Hotel remind us what country parks should not be about.

Finlaystone Estate

Langbank near Greenock Oct-Mar weekends only Apr-Sep daily until 5pm

Take the A8 to Greenock, Houston direction at Langbank, then signed from there. Finlaystone is the grand mansion home to Chief of Clan Macmillan and is set in formal gardens in a wooded estate. Lots of facilities ('Celtic' tearoom, craft shop, etc), leafy walks, walled garden. Rare magic.

Hirsel Country Park

Coldstream

On A697, north edge of town (direction Kelso). The 3000-acre grounds of Hirsel House (not open to the public). 2-4km walks through farmland and woods, including lovely, languid lake. Museum, tearoom and craft units at the Homestead.

The coast around the north of Scotland offers some of the best places in Europe from which to see whales and dolphins and, more ubiquitously, seals. You don't have to go on boat trips, though of course you get closer, the boatman will know where to find them and the trip itself can be exhilarating. Good operators are listed below. Dolphins are most active on a rising tide especially May-Sep.

Best in Scotland are the Moray and Cromarty Firths. The population of bottlenose dolphins in this area well exceeds 100 and they can be seen all year (though mostly Jun-Sep).

The Dolphins & Seals of the Moray Firth Centre

North of Kessock Bridge
01463 731866 or
01343 820339

Just north of the Kessock Bridge on the A9. Underwater microphones pick up the chatterings of dolphins and porpoises and there's always somebody there to explain. They keep an up-to-date list of recent sightings and all the cruises available. Summer only Mon-Sat 9.30am-4.30pm (closes for lunch 12.30-1pm).

Cromarty

Any vantage around town is good especially South Sutor for coastal walk and an old lighthouse cottage has been converted into a research station run by Aberdeen University. **Chanonry Point, Fortrose**, through the golf course, east end of point beyond lighthouse is the *best* place to see dolphins from land in Britain. Occasional sightings also at **Balintore**, opposite Seaboard Memorial Hall; **Tarbert Ness** beyond **Portmahomack**, end of path through reserve further out along the Moray Firth possible at **Burghead**, **Lossiemouth** and **Buckie**, **Spey Bay** and **Portknockie**. Also check the Dolphin Space Programme, an accreditation scheme for boat operators: www.dolphinspace.org

On the west coast, especially near Gairloch, you may sight orcas, dolphins and minke whales mainly in summer.

Rubha Reidh

Near Gairloch

20km north of Melvaig (unclassified road). Near Carn Dearg Youth Hostel west of Lonemore. Where road turns inland is a good spot.

Greenstone Point

North of Laide

Off A832 (unclassified road) through Mellon Udrigle round Gruinard Bay. Harbour porpoises Apr-Dec, minke whales May-Oct.

Red Point of Gairloch

Gairloch

By B8056 via Badachro round Loch Gairloch. High ground looking over North Minch and south to Loch Torridon. Harbour porpoises often along the coast.

Rubha Hunish

Skye

The far northwest finger of Skye. Walk from Duntulm Castle or Flodigarry. Dolphins and minke whales in autumn.

A few other locations also offer sightings.

Mousa Sound

Shetland

20km south of Lerwick.

Ardnamurchan

The Point

The most westerly point on this wildly beautiful peninsula. Go to end of road or park near Sanna Beach and walk round. Sanna Beach worth going to just to walk the strand. Visitor centre; tearoom.

Stornoway

Isle of Lewis

Heading out of town for Eye Peninsula, at Holm near Sandwick south of A866 or from Bayble Bay (all in walking distance).

St Abb's Head

Near Berwick
www.nlb.org.uk

9km north of Eyemouth and 10km east of main A1. Spectacular cliff scenery, a huge sea bird colony, rich marine life and varied flora. Good view from top of stacks, geos and cliff face full of serried ranks of guillemot, kittiwake, razorbill, etc. Hanging gardens of grasses and campion. Behind cliffs, grassland rolls down to the Mire Loch and its varied habitat of bird, insect, butterfly life and vegetation. The coffee shop at the car park does a mean scone.

Sands Of Forvie & The Ythan Estuary

Newburgh
www.jncc.gov.uk

25km north Aberdeen. Cross bridge outside Newburgh on A975 to Cruden Bay and park. Path follows Ythan estuary, bears north and enters the largest undisturbed dune system in the UK. Dunes in every aspect of formation. Collieston, a 17/18th-century fishing village, is 5km away. These habitats support the largest population of eiders in UK (especially Jun) and huge numbers of terns. It's easy to get lost here, so get lost!

Beinn Eighe

Torridon

Bounded by A832 south from Gairloch and A896 west of Kinlochewe, this first National Nature Reserve in Britain includes remaining fragments of old Caledonian pinewood on the south shore of Loch Maree (largest in West Highlands) and rises to the rugged tops with their spectacular views and varied geology. Excellent wood and mountain trails with starts on both roads: woodland strolls from A832 on Loch Maree side. Starts to the Beinn and to Liatach are from the A896 Glen Torridon road. Visitor centres on both roads.

John Muir Country Park

Dunbar
ECO

Vast park between Dunbar and North Berwick named after the Dunbar-born father of the conservation movement. It includes estuary of the Tyne and the park is also known as Tyninghame. Diverse habitats: cliffs, sand spits and woodland. Many bird species. Crabs, lichens, sea and marsh plants. Enter at east extremity of Dunbar at Belhaven, off the B6370 from A1; or off A198 to North Berwick 3km from A1. Or better, walk from Dunbar by cliff-top trail (2km+).

Lochwinnoch

Lochwinnoch
RSPB

30km southwest of Glasgow via M8 junction 28A then A737 past Johnstone onto A760. Also from Largs 20km via A760. The reserve is just outside the village on the lochside and comprises wetland and woodland habitats. A serious nature centre, incorporating an observation tower. Hides and marked trails; and a birds-spotted board. Shop and coffee shop. Events programme. Good for kids. Visitor centre open daily 10am-5pm.

Insh Marshes

Kingussie
RSPB

4km from town along B970 (past Ruthven Barracks), 2500 acres of Spey floodplain run by the RSPB. Trail (3km) marked out through meadow and wetland and a note of species to look out for (including 6 types of orchid, 7 'red list' birds and half the UK population of goldeneye). Also 2 hides (250m and 450m) high above marshes, vantage points to see waterfowl, birds of prey, otters and deer. The area was declared a National Nature Reserve in 2003.

Vane Farm

Loch Leven
ECO
RSPB
☕

RSPB reserve on south shore of Loch Leven, beside and bisected by B9097 off junction 5 of M90. Easily reached visitor centre with observation lounge and education/orientation facilities. Hide nearer loch side reached by tunnel under road. Nature trail on hill behind through heath and birchwood (2km circular). Good place to introduce kids to nature watching. Centre 10am-5pm. Hides always open. Events: 01577 862355.

Islay Wildlife Information & Field Centre

Port Charlotte
ECO

Jam-packed info centre that's very 'hands-on' and interactive. Up-to-date displays of geology, natural history (rocks, skeletons, sealife tanks). Recent-sightings-of-wildlife board, flora and fauna lists, video room, reference library. Great for kids – kids' area and activity days. Apr-Oct 10am-4pm. Closed Sat (Jun-Aug 10am-5pm 7 days).

Balranald

North Uist
RSPB

West coast of North Uist reached by the road from Lochmaddy, then the Bayhead turnoff at Clachan Stores (10km north). This most western, most faraway reach is one of the last redoubts of the disappearing corncrake. Catch its calling while you can.

Part 6

Scotland the best

Top 10s for 2010

Top 10 Edinburgh Restaurants

1 **Martin Wishart** One of only 2 restaurants with more than 2 ticks in *StB*. Coz it's the best. Handily, a stone's throw from my office in Leith.

2 **Number 1 Princes Street** Here No. 1 is not just an address. It is dear but damned fine.

3 **Urban Angel** Two easy-to-love café/bistros in the city centre. Manage to be both urban in atmos and angelic in their approach to food.

4 **Amore Dogs** The Italian version of the expanding litter of 'Dogs' diners. Great value and noise.

5 **Redwood** Fresh from California in old St Stephen Street where they still remember the Grateful Dead. Sunny, simple, light food. Scottish ingredients; pacific time.

6 **Iris** The 2010 secret spot in midtown. Iris just lowers her eyes when we say we adore to dine with her.

7 **La Cucina** Bold and brash Missoni style, the rock 'n' roll ristorante at the tacky end of the Royal Mile. Perfect if pricey pasta.

8 **Tail End** The mid-Leith Walk caff and takeaway with the lighter, fresher touch. You wait but you want to.

9 **Café Marlayne** In a city with more French restaurants than any other in the UK, this tiny bistro is simply *sans pareil*.

10 **Loopy Lorna's** Taking the tearoom into a new realm in the Miss Jean Brodie end of town, LL gets a VG++ from me

Top 10 Glasgow Restaurants

1 Ubiquitous Chip The longest-established restaurant on this page by a margin. As Glasgow's bastion of fine dining, the UC would be on anybody's top 10 list.

2 Martin Wishart at Cameron House Edinburgh's top – and Michelin – chef overseeing the elegant serene dining room of De Vere's remodeled Cameron House on Loch Lomond, outside the city.

3 Bistro Du Vin Compared to 'The Chip' this is a recent arrival, replacing previous restaurants in Glasgow's original boutique hotel. Effortlessly stylish.

4 Cafézique Neighbourhood café/bistro that's the off-shoot of the West End's most simpatico deli. Casual meet-and-eat doesn't come cooler than this.

5 Guy's Underestimated and my favourite Merchant City caff for eclectic eats. Lengthy menu; all good.

6 La Vallée Blanche Heart of Byres Road area, an upstairs room with great atmosphere and French flair.

7 The Two Figs New fig on the Byres Road block where there are many foodstops to choose from. Casual, contemporary caff and bistro; born to be loved.

8 Stravaigin All Stravaigins are tops but the street-level pub above the main restaurant excels for gastrogrub value and vibe.

9 City Merchant The defining Merchant City restaurant. Family-run, sound Scottish sourcing; totally reliable. Best choice near George Square.

10 Crabshakk The seafood shack that arrived in Glasgow's emerging foodie district west of west to immediate acclaim. And mine. Kill for a table!

Top 10 Best-Value Hotels

1 10 Hill Place, Edinburgh Not found in the style guides but this cool hotel on a quiet square by the university is a real find for you.

2 Six St Mary's Place, Edinburgh Friendly, 'ethical' B&B in boho Stockbridge. No frills but refreshingly realistic rates.

3 George Hotel, Inverary Old, family-run. Rooms quite chic; atmospheric bar, famous for food – all at no'-bad prices.

4 Ship Inn, Gatehouse of Fleet Renovated pub with rooms in charming GoF. Great base for Galloway gallivantings.

5 Royal Hotel, Comrie Town hotel of canny wee Comrie in the best bit of Perthshire for walk 'n' thought. Stylish. Good food; local bar.

6 Craigatin House, Pitlochry Contemporary and comfy guest house at end of the strip in this tourist town. *Muy ambiente.*

7 Fortingall House, Aberfeldy Country-estate hospitality and style near one of Scotland's grandest glens.

8 Lovat Arms, Fort Augustus Family-run contemporary hotel at foot of Loch Ness. Tourists go past – you should linger.

9 The Globe Inn, Aberdeen Inexpensive, pleasant rooms above a great pub in a city centre where deals are few.

10 Glenfinnan House Highland atmosphere, friendly people, a country house on Loch Shiel: the real hospitality.

Top 10 Pubs With ATMOS

1 Drover's Inn, Inverarnan The classic roadside hostelry seems unchanged since 1705 – dark, firelit, raucous: real.

2 Castlebay Hotel Bar, Barra Overlooking the said castle and bay. Great craic for islanders and visitors alike.

3 The Mishnish, Mull Legendary Tobermory quayside bar in same family forever. All things to a' folks. Drink the atmos.

4 The Ceilidh Place, Ullapool One of the most sociable, creative and life-affirming, all-purpose places in these Highlands.

5 Clachaig Inn, Glencoe Deep in the glen, the definitive after-the-hill spot to descend on: crowded, universal, vital.

6 The Ship Inn, Elie Great for grub but much more. Hub of the village with outside terrace on tranquil Elie beach and lagoon.

7 Scotia Bar, Glasgow Intimate, historic, city-centre pub, a den of drinking, music, craic and culture since yon times.

8 Òran Mór, Glasgow Converted church on a prominent corner of the West End; pubs/theatre/club/bistros, all celebrating Glasgow life.

9 Café Royal, Edinburgh Classic, lofty, Victorian watering-hole and oyster bar; atmos built in with the mirrors and tiles.

10 Port o' Leith, Edinburgh Created in recent memory by one Mary Moriarty; the epitome of a worldly yet neighbourhood tavern.

Top 10 Away Days With Kids

1 Crieff Hydro Scotland's favourite family hotel resort where everyone can play. Prodigious menu of distractions.

2 Calgary Farmhouse Hotel, Mull Laid-back hotel/gallery/bistro in rare woods with art/adventure trail.

3 Drumlanrig, Thornhill House with art and courtyard of things but also huge grounds to explore, especially by bike.

4 Cromarty, Black Isle Seaside village perfect for kids with walks and caffs and usually dolphins.

5 Auchrannie, Arran Extensive hotel annex built for families for day or stay. Pools and ploys and outdoors, there's Arran.

6 Falls of Bruar, Blair Atholl Waterfall and woodland walks away from the supershop emporium on the A9. Relief from retail.

7 Edinburgh Zoo, Edinburgh Your kids and their animals staring at each other in wonder... A world-class family attraction.

8 Cream o' Galloway, Rainton An eco-activity-and-adventure park based on the irresistible allure of their ice cream.

9 Kelburn, Largs Attraction-stuffed grounds of mansion near Largs; Millport and Cumbrae a wee ferry away. Nardini's ice cream on the way home.

10 Loch Insh, Kincraig Lochside centre (stay or visit) in scenic Rothiemurchus with range of cool activities on and off water.

Top 10 Romantic & Bittersweet Scotland

1 Glencoe Few roads anywhere are as dramatic as the A82 through the most impressive of glens: history and geography, the ridge and the mountains.

2 Rosslyn Chapel, Roslin A church so steeped in human mystery and romance that it can be hard to even think of God.

3 Dryburgh Abbey Of all the Border abbeys with their history of glory and gore, this remains in its stones and situation the epitome of romance.

4 Culloden A battleground and story veiled in tears powerfully demonstrates the enduring fascination of that doomed cause.

5 Kildrummy Castle, Alford The most evocative of Highland castle ruins with a gorgeful of gardens besides.

6 The Italian Chapel, Orkney Hard to leave without a tear in the eye. A touching statement of faith made so far from home.

7 Dunvegan Castle, Skye The location, the Fairy Flag and the gardens to the mystic shore all combine to fuel our romantic imagination.

8 Grave of Flora Macdonald, Skye Scotland's most romantic heroine whose mass funeral here showed she was a Di of her day.

9 Balquhidder Churchyard Not just Rob Roy's grave but the whole setting and the viewpoint above suffuse you with Scottishness.

10 The Road to the Isles The A830 between Glenfinnan and Mallaig takes you through the magnificent heart of Bonnie Prince Charlie country.

Top 10 Places For Contemplation

1 Pluscarden Abbey, Elgin Medieval Benedictine monastery in inspiring spot. You can stay or simply attend their many services.

2 Angus's Garden, Taynuilt Extensive, partly wild private garden around a loch in memory of a lost son. A calm contemplative corner of Argyll.

3 Loch an Eilean, Rothiemurchus Perfect Highland loch. By no means a secret but large enough in circumference for meditative meanderings.

4 Iona Abbey The ancient cradle of Christianity on tiny Iona where it is always mild. An active community but built for personal enlightenments.

5 Jura House Gardens, Jura Amongst the many gardens in Scotland, this is so remote you may have it to yourself; an island on an island of perfect tranquillity.

6 Graveyards in Edinburgh There are many and not just in the Old Town where one can wander and ponder on the history of an ancient influential city.

7 The Angus Glens There are three, all with different characters but easy to find yourself in. Strolls, hikes and views aplenty. A civilised back-of-beyond.

8 Castle Tioram & Ardnamurchan The enigmatic ruin in a dreamy spot but the whole of this peninsula, from bare hills to ancient woodlands, is balm for the soul.

9 The Brown and White Caterhuns, Edzell Iron Age remains on hillocks that look into prehistory and the Highlands where one can sense our place in it all.

10 The Commando Monument, Spean Bridge A prominent and much-visited crossroads. Consider the nobility and the sacrifice of a soldier's life in all wars.

Scot land the best

'The only guide worth a damn'
The Scotsman

Available from all good bookshops.

Or order your complete copy of *Scotland the Best*
from the HarperCollins Hotline on: 0870 787 1724,

or write to:

Customer Services,
HarperCollins Publishers,
Westerhill Road,
Bishopbriggs,
Glasgow G64 2QT

enclosing a cheque made payable to
HarperCollins Publishers.

Free P & P for all UK orders.
Please allow 14 days for delivery.